VITAL RECORDS

poems by

Joycelyn Trigg

Finishing Line Press
Georgetown, Kentucky

VITAL RECORDS

Copyright © 2025 by Joycelyn Trigg
ISBN 979-8-88838-978-2 First Edition
All rights reserved under International and Pan-American Copyright Conventions. No part of this book may be reproduced in any manner whatsoever without written permission from the publisher, except in the case of brief quotations embodied in critical articles and reviews.

ACKNOWLEDGMENTS

My gratitude to the editors of the following publications in which versions of these poems appeared:

Borders: "That's My Girl"

Calyx: "Punch"

Minerva Rising: "Daddy's Girl," "For My Father"

Persephone's Daughters: "Family Story"

Talking River: "Impersonator," "Manmade"

Deep thanks also to Cathy Bowers, without whom these poems would never have been written; Cynthia Wall, for accompanying and encouraging me as she watched this book happen; Peggy Shumaker, Greg Glazner, and Kevin Goodan for their excellence, guidance, and generosity as mentors at the Ranier Writing Workshop; for Westwords, my local writing group, and Tea and Poetry, a local poetry study group; Indigo Moor, poet friend, for walking with me all the way to publication; and Alan Peters for his patience with hearing these "stories" over and over.

Publisher: Leah Huete de Maines
Editor: Christen Kincaid
Cover Art: Shutterstock
Author Photo: Joycelyn Trigg
Cover Design: Elizabeth Maines McCleavy

Order online: www.finishinglinepress.com
also available on amazon.com

Author inquiries and mail orders:
Finishing Line Press
PO Box 1626
Georgetown, Kentucky 40324
USA

Contents

I
Your Last Dance 1
Incurable 3
Family Story 5
My Mother's Doll 7
Backdrop 8
Punch 9
Preview 10

II
Innocence 13
Never 14
Love, Interrupted 16
The Master Story 18
Ellis 20
The Key 21
Acting 22

III
Trumpet Sounding on Joliet Street 25
Miscarriage 26
Daddy's Girl 28
For My Mother 29
Cracks 30
Night Vision 32

IV
For My Father 35
Apprentice 36
Past Sweetness 39
Last Words 41
That's My Girl 42
My Daughter Finally Moves Out 44

V
If Only 47
Reflection 48
How to Live Alone 49

When No One Comes to Visit 50
After You Left 51
Audubon Park 53
Moonbow 54
Impersonator 55
Going Back to Mississippi 57
Calling 59
I Take It Back 61
For Once 64
Leavings 65

   VI
Manmade 69

Let us all be from somewhere.
Let us tell each other everything we can.
　　　Bob Hicok, "A Primer"

*For
Luke and Melissa,
who understand poetic license*

I

Your Last Dance

was the first
time you strolled
into Mississippi, to music
you rode from New Orleans
streets on Friday nights
when your neighborhood forgot
it had only bread for supper,
kicked off what shoes it had,
and declared itself a party.

The room you entered
was square and bare.
Fiddlers crooned their mating call.
A line of cleaned-up country boys
leaned against the wall.
You and your red dress swayed
into the room and took its breath away.

You in high heels, dark hair dancing,
Cajun eyes scanning, landing on *him*.
Everybody breathed. The music
started up again, and the friend you came with
named the boys gathering around.
And him? you asked
of the handsome one hanging back,
looking from you to the door.

You made his choice
for him. You crossed the room
and took his hand: Dance
with me? No way for you
to know he'd never danced before,
and tonight behind his Baptist mama's back.
No way for him to know dancing
was the way you moved through the world
never quite touching down
on the hard, sharp ground.

No way to know what it would cost
when you left that room together,
where the whole story
of your long, dissonant lives,
and mine,
had just been written.

Incurable

As if in a photo, gray Lake Pontchartrain,
gray the train car that carries us
away, and gray my small self
standing alone, back to the window and the water
trembling, too, at what has just been done,
this leaving of a child to strangers.

For us, our mother will say,
for my brother Billy and me,
as if it were a gift to be alone with her
grief and guilt that began
when our brother John's birth went wrong
and now breaches the levees.
None of us will escape the Home for Incurables,
not even my father, who would have no part of this
and waits at home with the empty playpens
for the news that she has really done it.

I am one baby too many
after all those years of carrying John
while only his body grew.
Surely Billy would agree
one of us had to go.

Year after year
my father holds my hand tight
every time we face the aging building.
Inside, the impossible
stairs past old men wandering,
the baby with the giant head,
the woman shaking the tall bars of her bed,
to the small screened porch where they bring John,
hands tied to the wooden arms of his wheelchair,
his back to the house and ours
to the world as we encircle him.

At night we try to sleep
at my grandparents' duplex, the old
linoleum cool and sticky to my face
on the floor, where I lie watching
Morgus the Magnificent
and waiting for the bell
of the ice cream truck.

I am the one left
after John: left
on the bench on the train
while my mother's arms ride
empty. That is all I see: No one
wears a red scarf. No one
calls for tickets. My mother does not
cry. I have no brothers. I see
only me, observed from outside it all,
having just learned that trick
that will serve me, sometimes
well, all my life.

Family Story
    for my mother

The girl runs faster
than the mother's thick legs after her
past the sign neither can read,
the girl not yet—some
hard word like Carondelet or Xavier—
the mother, never. The girl
trusts her thin, mosquito-bit legs
slashing the air
like stilettos on tires

and does not look back
at the mother stopped, cursing
her from the street she dare not cross for fear
she will not know the signs
home. She waits for the girl just inside,
her first lash on those bare legs masked
by the slam of the screen door,
the next their own hard cracks

until the girl slides under the bed
where her little brother waits, shaking.
The cat-o'-nine-tails scrapes
cool linoleum, scratching
like cat's claws. The girl thinks
Mama cannot reach us here, cannot
imagine all our places to run or hide.

The brother pees his pants.
The girl lets her skirt soak it up
and in its warmth they fall
asleep until the father's heavy steps
and the rattling of milk bottles
left from his day's route wake them.
They hear the mother
in the kitchen curse
the girl again in Cajun French,

bad girl, disobedient, refusing
even to let her poor brother out
from under the bed for supper.
The father drags a low chair to the bed,
bends to remove his sturdy boots
so close the girl can hear his teeth clench,
then rises and answers: Tell me first.
What you are making us?

My Mother's Doll

She is the center
of your room, the dark beauty
that man picked up in Texas
said she looked too much like you
to resist. I stand beside you
invisible in the mirror where I see
your eyes find her,
go soft and dreamy and
twitch with something unfamiliar.
I want to lie in bed beside her, just once
be the one to make you smile.

Backdrop

Single file like a string
pulled by the teacher down
the hall on oily wooden floors,
to the stairs behind the stage
where the photographer waited
among looming curtains,
a single bright light
bare as an interrogator's
on the seat he would lift
us to one by one. Teasing
and tickling, he got each child
smiling. He got what he wanted
for their mothers.

I would not climb the stairs.
"We'll see," you had said,
and a little child thought
you meant, "I'll see you,"
believed you understood
my fear, would come
keep me safe,
as I had cried for you to do.

But as the line got shorter
and shorter, they would not
let me wait any longer.
It took two of them to tug me
last up the dark stairs
to the hard glare, the waiting chair.
They did not try
to cheer me. I looked around
for you one last time
but all I saw past
the stairwell was a window
framing empty sky.

Punch

In a circle of folding
chairs, the church women settle,
come from town
for my mama's punch.

Among them, I
wait, too, feet dangling,
thirsty, having long before
been kicked out of the kitchen,

where she still stirs and pours
to please these women
who suspect both
her beauty and her birthplace.

Don't ever tell, she had told me,
as I watched her
scrub the bucket, the only thing
she has to hold so much.

I cannot resist: "Miss Nola,"
I whisper, "Mama
mixed the punch in a bucket."
The room turns

on her, framed in the doorway,
offering a crystal bowl
full of sweet, green drink,
her eyes on mine.

Preview

Familiar whistle, and cue
the car door closing. The little girl
settling for play on the cool floor,
her mother washing dishes,
jumps up and out.
Daddy's home.

Running down the porch stairs
she sees him golden, like a lamp
on her picture book.
He pats his shirt pocket,
holds out his arms.
All her arms and legs jump into them
and hold like branches on the tree
over the river that taught her to swim.
The candy wrapper rustles,
and he presents to her
the cardboard paten of Coconut Huts
they break apart and serve each other.

Inside, her mother takes her time with the dishes,
carries on as she has done all week.
Friday nights in the dark, this.
Monday mornings in the dark, gone.

Run to him, she always tells the girl.
Wouldn't any mother? But tonight,
as she watches them kneel together
in the light the house pours for them
and overhears the secret
language of their laughter,
she wonders what she has started.

II

Innocence

At 15, walking apart
from our friends on dusty roads,
you gathered honeysuckle,
wove it into a crown
you placed on my hair long enough

your fingertips fondled the end of it
as it spilled onto your desk
behind mine in economics class
while your other hand
took notes. Mine
traced your initials over and over

while I squirmed at your touch
until I had to add my own.

Never

Ricky driving, Linda hugging her door.
In the backseat you held

my still-smooth hand, gently
rubbed it in circles like a lamp

for luck. As we turned
toward home the radio sang

Never, My Love.
And I believed.

The four of us
between the drive-in and the fire tower

forever. You
hadn't kissed me yet.

We would never run
out of time,

it could wait,
let it wait like a light in a window

that would welcome us home.
The others were already there

when we stopped,
cars parked

here and there, couples dissolving
into the group or the night.

You and I ran
to the top of the fire tower holding on

to the sturdy rails
cool and damp with the fall night

all the way up into the waiting
arms of the breeze.

In the moonlight
we saw the familiar

land to the end of the horizon.
Saw no end

to the stars lighting
the sky.

Below was empty now
except for Ricky and Linda

leaning against his parents' Caprice,
Linda hugging herself.

We all thought we had time
for waiting.

Love, Interrupted

Sunday afternoons, crowded
into Don's souped-up Chevy,
we rode the back roads we knew
like blood knows veins.

This last Sunday of summer
we met up at Coach's house
for early football on TV.
The right front

room was a bedroom.
You and I sat on the bed,
laughing. Coach called popcorn
and one by one

the others went into the living
room where the game was on.
You and I stayed. I laid
my head on your shoulder,

you stroked my hair, lifted my face,
kissed me, gentle
as the waiting, hard
as the wanting what seemed ours.

We took our places beside each other,
as if we knew what we were doing,
my hand catching yours then letting it go
simply to rest at my waist, holding

the twin hands of my heart
and our children reaching from the future
as if longing were enough
to make it so. I wanted you.

I never told you
why I then rode off the next weekend
with the Burden boys when they drove in
from Florida with their convertible top down.

Ask the ghost of my best friend
pressed that day like newsprint against the window screen.
When I closed my eyes, kissing you
I saw her too, innocent of speeding trucks,

her brown eyes locked on mine
as I almost began to live
right there in front of her
wanting that could never be enough.

The Master Story
>   *for Linda Ann*

In that one normal fall
spent giggling over the party
line, we stole a night, lit
a pocket in it, the two of us,
a flashlight, and Peyton Place
under the sheets, turning
the pages, our faces
whispering the forbidden
stories, forgotten now—but not you,

too soon taken out
at the junction of leaving
town and a highway going north,
which I cannot help but travel,
nor can 18-wheelers like the one
you met. On the first day of Christmas break
I answered the phone expecting you
to tell me what we would do
with so much time. The call took you away
and me into my deepest black
and white nightmare of waking
to find Earth entirely abandoned
except for me, alone
with cans of beans and tuna
I swore would be enough.

For Christmas, you were buried
wearing a pearl ring, black and white,
that my cousin planned to give you, more
than the popcorn on drive-in double dates
you ate to stall his intentions.
I wanted only to sit with you again
all night beneath a sheet of light,
wanted you to tell me what I could do
now, what could go on
without you. I never had a chance.

I left my first love
for fear the phone wouldn't ring
or that it would. Then my second.
Now a new love, unknowing, offers a ring
like yours, waits at the door.

Ellis

She remembers you
walking toward her
in your white shirt, khaki pants, gray vest,
handsome through the screen
door of her parents'
duplex on Joliet Street,

then how your breath smelled of booze,
and her heart beat fast
for all the wrong reasons. She turned
you away and now, after all,
it is the moment just before that
she recalls, what you exchanged

outside her door, before she closed it.
Forget the rest
of us. She asks for this one thing,
that I find the photo of you buried
in the box unearthed when we emptied her
house last summer.

I will get to it soon enough
for her, I hope. I have to
get ready to excavate the layers
of faces, mostly hers, between her
at eighteen, making such a choice,

now at eighty-eight wanting only that
moment back. Do you
really think it is you she wants?
Or to be eighteen, maybe
even to refuse you again,
to know such power,

such turning
she must have called hope,
before learning that
for what came after,
she could never quite
open the door again.

The Key

A night in New Orleans, 1938.
A double date. The boy's name forgotten
but a memory of stopping

the old Packard at a bridge
and trips to the bathroom.
You and the other girl,

named something innocent like Jane,
listened through the bathroom walls
to the boys talk. When you heard

what they intended, you
slipped off your heels and ran to the car.
Found the key. To Jane's amazement

you tossed it in the river, opened
your face to the bold moonlight,
and led the way home.

Acting

Two couples out for a Sunday drive,
the jeep top down. Wind blowing too much

to resist, the woman in front stood
and waved, laughing, calling out

as if from a Mardi Gras float.
The others laughed too,

except the driver, embarrassed by her,
never having been to Mardi Gras

and not one to pretend.
Sit down, he growled. Quit

acting like a child.
Decades later she lay in a hospital bed.

As the surgeon left her room laughing
her son came in and caught her laughing too.

Stop that, he scolded: Quit
acting silly at a time like this.

The next day they installed a pacemaker.
Later she cried

over what my brother had said,
how it made her feel

the way she did that day in the jeep.
Then she laughed. Maybe,

she said, they'll be satisfied
if this thing really does regulate my heart.

III

Trumpet Sounding on Joliet Street

Night jasmine blooms below the open window.
Grandpa pours evening drinks.
Daddy pours his own on the plant near his chair
when Grandpa leaves the room. My mother
throws a glance at him that cracks like ice.
The air is thick and wet, a film
binding us the way my brother does,
a not-so-still point across town at The Home
around which these visits turn.
Next door, the neighbor, while his mother wails,
plays his trumpet low and long.

Next time we visit, I hear Grandpa say that
he is gone, the man next door, a gunshot.
The mother taken away.
The jasmine lingers
too sweet. The loose, dark earth
it stands in—how soft it must feel.

Miscarriage

I envy this family
of deer living in my woods
crossing the yard single file
at dusk. See how they know each other
and in what order
they process. This evening
the second young one turned and waited
for another, taking her rightful place.
I say her because today
I have missed you,
the sister I imagine,
who would have been
the oldest daughter. I
lived in your place, behind
our broken brother, or should I say
where he was meant to live. I moved
from second—or was it third?—to first.
You see my confusion.

You were barely mentioned,
you know—nothing personal.
In that first grief's shadow you,
and I, dimmed. Even now
our mother believes
John would have been handsome
and (who knows?) the brightest

if not for long labor and the old nurse
wanting only to put on her blue sweater
and walk into the spring night
toward sleep. Instead
she clamped her chilly arms around our mother's tired legs
when the time came, pausing everything
as if it were no more than a movie,
until the doctor returned from supper.

If grief is a color it must be
brown like old blood. It is
the color of the house I was born into.
If grief is a name, it became our family's.
Daddy bore it to his grave. Mother dug herself
a kind of cave in the back room
where she took in other mothers' children,
papered the walls with pictures,
outlines they drew:
a woman, children, a room
like empty boxes.

It was not right-
fully mine to do, but I tried
to make it up to them. I gave everything.
To Daddy, who left her in that room
and sat down with me to supper.
To every other room in the house—
open windows and their secret pleasure
of blue and green, sometimes
white on the tail of a deer,
or even true red on the lips of a female cardinal
aspiring from brown.
To her, a trophy daughter
perfect, nearly, enough
to prove it was not her fault. I was
all they had then. It should have been
you. And I would have thanked you
for taking my place, I think.

Daddy's Girl

In the curve of your arm
on the third pew as on every Sunday
that day I sat resting as if beneath a giant
branch stretched over a river,
kicking my feet in its cool water
until you said to stop or else,
and then once more.

Back home you proved
your word was good
and took me petticoats and all
to the back room.
I closed my eyes, breathed
Sunday dinner waiting,
heard the buckle click
like a key in a lock,
your belt hiss
as it leaped out.

You never struck me again,
a silent promise. I sat still
when you were watching.
We understood each other after that, always
knowing we could make the other
choice and lose each other in an instant
the way a single lightning bolt
can break the heart of a tree.

For My Mother

One of us says your name
and the sound of it stops
you midturn in the doorway,
like the gypsy dancer
on the music box
unwound in your room.
You would like hearing
you remind me of her,
so I won't tell you.

Or I'll tell you how
I watched you once
when I was small
hold her close
to your dresser mirror
to dance, two of her,
two of you, one of
me unseen among so many
trinkets at the bottom of the glass.

Now from across the room
I look at you again and listen
though I'd rather not hear
the song again, the lullaby you tossed
with the swing of your dark hair
into my baby bed. *Give me
land lots of land under starry skies above
don't fence me in* . . .

You sang and danced
when he wasn't looking. Now,
as if some nail has snagged your skirt,
you hesitate. You do
not recognize the door you stand in,
the voice that called you
back. You wait, as if you see both
before and after this
half step we've caught you in,
and you still think you have a choice
which way to go.

Cracks

No money in 1929,
but somehow Grandpa managed
many suppers of beans and rice

and day-old French bread to buy you
the golden-haired china doll
you begged for. All day

you held her close, armful of light
against your dark hair, arms
you told her would never let go.

But you tripped and fell
face down on the sidewalk,
both of you.

One other indulgence, first
heels and stockings not pencil-drawn,
a new dress shining like your face.

For your first date, New Orleans was raining.
You, running to the streetcar, caught
your heel on a crack, fell, everything ruined.

I married a penniless poet
who took an oil-rig job
to prove his manhood, lost

his soul and us somewhere over
the hungry Gulf at night, a chasm wide
open like the mouths of bayou alligators.

Living there, my little son
would pull his hand from mine
and drop to crawl every time

we came to a wide crack in the sidewalk.
Bending beside him,
I saw it too—

the turned row of dark earth,
the green fingers curling
invitations to fall.

Night Vision

Last night bright
shadows of branches lay

like cords around Luke
sleeping. He pushed

against them the way
I first felt

him move inside
me a year ago. I wanted

to remind you, tried
to wake you. You

apologized for something,
rolled over. I closed the curtains

and turned, lying again
with you in our smooth darkness,

where the knotted shadows
seemed no more

than pencil lines
morning would erase.

IV

For My Father

Dusk spreads like a shawl
around you sitting in the lawn chair,
newspaper twisted in your lap, eyes closed.
My son points to you, wanting
his favorite game. We
sneak up on you. Your hands
unfold to hold him.

Your hands damp
washed almost soft, almost clean.
You explained, mechanic's grease
won't come off. Your fingerprints
etched in black, I'd know them anywhere.

Luke calls for birds. You
point to one last martin
licking the day's rim for insects.
Then the black ground closes
around you.

       The two of you
become mere shapes beneath its folds.
I turn on the porch light
to hide the color it will be
when you are gone.

Apprentice

One last thing, my father says:
Let's go again to where we lived
young and innocent
and so, happy. One last time
to Pennsylvania, a place of plenty
work in summer, always
things to mend, friends
who still send cards and gifts
south to us winged by postmarks
exotic as Eden.

He and I went once before,
for him to show me the fall
leaves bright like party pastries
and the place where I first saw snow.
We lingered in Amish country,
his eyes spilling with envy
though his livelihood depends on machines.

In his shop back home
I sit at a greasy desk figuring accounts
while joint by aching joint
he tends every aging Volkswagen
from miles around. I hear him laugh
with college professors who can't check their oil.
I see him try to teach my brother the trade
but throw aside every wrong wrench.
Neither of us can imagine
a girl might learn such things.

The desk looks out on a single tree
dropping its sweet gum balls
like punching tickets for parking in its shade.
Black oil scars the desk like graffiti.
Oil on the tool bench, inside the fan, under
my father's fingernails so deep it goes to church with him.

With my greasy pencil I keep a record—
the symptoms, the costs, sometimes the pay—
in the simple way he has devised. I drive away
not knowing this wrench from that one.
But I can tell you the sound of a Barq's Root Beer
rattling its way through the old Coke box
into my hands in a cold sweat.

The summer my father will die
we go north again
to grant his wish. I go too,
in case. In the backseat of the van
my mother and young daughter
sit in their contentment with each other.
I ride beside him, sharing peppermint and peanuts,
feeling each sway of the camper
and the way his expert hands play
the steering wheel like an instrument.
He will drive every mile.

Once there he sets out again,
to replace a broken camper part. Another
sixty miles each way for the only one around.
Later I find him on the carport
sitting on the bumper of the van, staring
into his hands. Broken, he says.

I reach in as for my stub of pencil
and take the faulty part in my own hands.
The lawnmower next door shuts down.
The phone stops ringing.
I hold my breath
at such a risk: Two broken
parts, I mutter. Only
you could do this, but could you
take from each to make what you need?
I go inside and join the women
for lemonade, wanting a long walk and a cigarette.

The home-trip south takes no more
time than the trip north, enough for me
to try a new migraine medicine,
take that long walk at a campground,
finish reading *Bird by Bird,*
and break the last peppermint in two.

Past Sweetness

We celebrated April,
the month of your birth,
with fresh coconut cake,

your favorite. I
realize now
you couldn't taste it,

thanks to the chemo. No
wonder you look so defeated
in the photos.

I thought maybe
you knew what we did: this
you would not live to do again.

August would come, the true end
of the year. Outside the window
you lay near, pine trees rusting,

heat and humidity breeding
love bugs and hurricanes
that could leave us powerless for weeks,

the summer swelling,
splitting, peeling away,
burst to cracking

like the neighbor's dry pond bed
one year, mapping
a place no one wants to go.

You liked October best, and in your last
as Luke drove us toward you and Melissa slept
I thought of how many times

we had stood back of the house
under that tree near the pump house
and you cut sugarcane for me

and later for my children,
how that would never happen
again. My throat tightened

in a fist of aching
at the ways I would miss you.
What I would give for one more time.

But then there you were,
walking toward the car
as we pulled into the drive,

the purple cane stalk held out
like a pointer toward your grin.
"Surprised you, didn't I?" Yes,

again. With no other word between us
we followed around the house to what
by then was only a stump.

Your small, sharp pocket knife
I would know in a lineup
expertly scored a ring around a joint,

stripped the peel to fall like more dark leaves,
and cut pieces you passed to us
in this odd communion. You and I still

could say nothing, while the children chattered.
You held one piece in your hand.
When I looked from it to you,

you closed your hand around it,
having already lost your taste
for such hard sweetness.

Last Words
> *for my father*

Long past wanting, past fearing
the tall rider on a white horse
who really did seem to come
right into the room for you,

you lay still. In the low moan
of the air conditioner
in the August heat,
we wove in and out, slowly

untying the threads
that held you
to us, until finally
it was just you and me,

the way I wanted it.
You roused, and I rushed
to say the prescribed, unthinkable
words—that it was okay

for you to die. We would be
all right. I would.
You shook your head,
urgent. I insisted,

Yes, we would.
Then the moment was gone
for good, my lie
still echoing. My whole life

I waited for a word from you
that might set me free,
and when it came
I would not let you speak it.

That's My Girl
> *for my daughter*

The weatherman insists: rain.
Our hearts are set
on sun and sand, lazy waves.
Your small face lifts to mine,
and if a three-year-old could arch an eyebrow,
you did: *Well?*

I laugh, How can anybody know
what will happen? The worst
will be ice cream in the car
with the windows rolled up.

But we find bright sun, enough to satisfy
my need for a deep breath and yours
for dancing on this old yellow quilt
stitched with sand.

I tell you my story of coming here
with school friends for our annual sunburn
the first day of spring break.
One of those summers
a storm so big it had a name
rearranged it all, this manmade
beach now finger-marked by raking.

What was its name? you ask.
Camille. Say it loud
and you can hear the wind and water
crying, don't you think?
That almost-arch of the eyebrow again.
Maybe it was saying, Come here!

Behind us, cars glare on Highway 90
like shrimp heads on a platter.
Ahead, water all the way to the sky.

Off like a bird, *Over there!*
you sing, pointing to the horizon.
I want to go over there!

Come here! I call and chase you
back to the edge
for you to also see the patient reaching
of the Gulf, in case
it keeps you from your own.

My Daughter Finally Moves Out

After she returned from another summer in Mississippi
playing with her cousins, we walked the Chattahoochee River trail where
she found me a jewel of orange lichen on a finger of brown bark.

After she walked too far ahead to the night water's hum,
staying between the lines the moon-stitched Gulf wove on the sand,
I gave her nightmares, a sea monster calling her name.

After she saw a geode split into its white flesh, every rock was mystery
staying in a fishbowl she hugged through all our moves.
She gave it down to me from the attic to hold for the next one.

After Hurricane Katrina moved up Highway 49 to her grandmother's,
staying meant hiding from the plague of love bugs that came next.
I gave her *courage* written all over a shawl big enough for both of them.

After I left for travel forgetting a proper goodbye
she called, leaving home, her voice trembling over the loose connection.
She gave me one last guilt trip.

After years of long black hair doodling the bathtub,
after piles of clothes furnished her room,
she gave one last look around and left
after putting my house in order.

V

If Only

The mother folds her arms
like a cradle for the child she lost,
not this one.

When the child cries at night
the mother calls out, *There's no one
there.* She's right.

The little boy ignores the burger
his mother bought him, until she says,
If you love me, eat every bite.

Reflection

My phone becomes a mirror

                                        my mother

my son on the line
holding up the glass.

Mirror, Mirror, who is not there
for him? I see

                                        Medusa

he has always needed me
to know: I never knew
I had no ears. All tongues,

                                        warning

deaf to the silence
that is how he asks for blessing,

                                        I am

always tightly coiled to strike

                                        poison

the love of my life.

How to Live Alone

I live in deep woods where deer
eat the forsythia within
three days of its bright blooming

and once ate the calla lilies I planted
to help me imagine thriving
in a coastal town across the continent—

I have not moved. Not
to mention the way the fig tree
fed its leaves like salad to the deer,

now bears its fruit
for apparently invisible
birds quicker to dip than I to see.

In the shadow
of the tall trees around my house,
grass has left the yard to moss.

Ferns in early spring,
question marks along my driveway
as if reconsidering, spring

so hot it already feels like summer
except the trees have no leaves
to slow the wind that burns

all illusion. Last night on my deck
guests whispered about wanting
to borrow my truck but the tank was empty.

They stayed just long enough
to drink exactly as many beers
as I left them cold.

When No One Comes to Visit

he sits right there in your favorite chair.
You remember, the one with the foot rest

under the good lamp by the window.
He has nothing to say for himself

when I ask him where he's been,
what he wants of me.

It's the silent treatment
in a voice just like yours,

holding his breath lest I mistake it for a sigh,
pretending he's not there

when I offer him a drink, coffee, me.
I guess what's coming, the stir

of air as he shifts in the chair,
rises, leaves without a word.

I should have known it's still too soon,
that I would pick another man just like you.

After You Left

It rained
and the river's skin turned brown
and smooth like a woman's
bare arm reaching.
In the forgiving light of fireflies
she was beautiful. This way,

the fireflies pointed, and glad
for their company I followed
along the trail, past the small rapids
where the heron first showed me
how to catch a fish
with one sure stroke of a blue pen.

Past one pink mushroom
and early blackberries like erasers on the vines.
To the small bridge over the stream
crawling toward the river
like a child toward home. There

the fireflies left,
and dark shoved me
back. Your absence slammed like a door,
and I ran, knowing what waited,
roots like ropes to trap

me there, dreading most
the narrow place where tangled vines
grow thick and sharp, and dark
hides things hungry too soon
for the sweetness of the not
ripe berries and honeysuckle.

I ran on, remembered
to breathe once and then again
breathed in the surprise of unseen blooms
as if your hand just brushed mine
passing in a room
and no one knows but me.

Fear ran on alone. Reaching deep
into the vines I pulled them to me
as I would you if you were here. Then
I walked, a slow, deliberate walk
through the dark, longing
etched on my arms.

Audubon Park

It is late
afternoon when we leave our room
in the bed and breakfast just off the park
for a walk among the joggers.
We are sated with holding
back from desire for
some reason that hardly seems
good enough, and with
gumbo and po-boys.

The park is emptying,
the light going gray
when we stop beside
a lake so tiny it seems spilled
around an island stuffed
with trees. They shudder
and hum, flash with white, go

still. More egrets come and settle
in the branches. And more
and more. I am astonished
how such light can choose
to contain itself,
let darkness have its moment.

Moonbow

It has been a hard summer for us,
of gathering and scattering
the would-be love between us
that feels too hungry for me.
We sit silent in the dark
on the steps of the cabin,
listening to the Toccoa whisper
its flowing just yards away
and watching a full moon climb the sky.
Then you recall Cumberland Falls
and how, on clear nights like this one,
the moon plays with the spray of the falls
and makes a moonbow.
I look at you and say,
It would be crazy. You
say, But shall we?

We drive through the night
to see the moon reigning
the midnight sky,
and the white arc of light
across the falls, as if
the moon has waved a wand
and left a glow. We stand in
this brightness I would have missed
if not for you. Then
we walk the moonlit trails
back to the car and you drive again
into the night, my face
pressed against my window to watch
the wild moon swerving and winding
to show us the only way home.

Impersonator

The first one stood out
of a limo sunroof in Helen, Georgia,
in an afternoon parade

that got in my way. Elvis dead
friendly, tall, waving
the whole time we idled in our cars

in a southern mountain town pretending
it was Germany. It was not
what I expected. I laughed

at the figure resurrected
between Atlanta and a rendezvous at Unicoi
with a long secret love.

In Jackson, Mississippi, I saw
the real thing once, sweaty
then too, in a different light.

I went with my mother and her friend,
who later also became so fat
she died. For love

of a man she couldn't have. I
will not. I went for the fun,
one last chance

to see my old junior-high crush
three-dimensional. Elvis
was a mountain, covered in white,

shadowed in blue, the color
of shoes, Christmas, scarves
another Elvis served like communion

at the nursing home to my mother,
on his knees beside her wheelchair
begging her to love him

tender. He gave
her a hug and the scarf
she spread out over her

one small drawer, shading
old makeup and perfume, country music CDs,
photos of grandchildren, everything

blue. She cried
as he sang of love,
what she still longed for, the world

of wanting and waiting, like me
in my car in Helen, my lover at Unicoi,
that held up everything.

Going Back to Mississippi

Ivy gropes the old
brick walls where I sit in the sun
with a beer named Rogue, just
blocks from my mother
napping in the nursing home.

I came a long way
yesterday, spent
today planning for her last days
in a dining room
smoky with catfish frying.
A baby grand sang.
If only she were
still a femme fatale lounging there.

At this unfamiliar bar
I breathe a little
car exhaust, leftover cigarettes,
gardenia blooms beyond the patio
walls. I settle myself into a wrought
iron chair and crackled shade
sketched by ivy
and the probing sun.

I am tempted to close my eyes.
But I might fall asleep, might dream,
might wake to find
nothing has changed.
I take a drink, check
my lipstick, my calendar,
my phone for the call
that will come soon.

When I look up,
everything has changed
as if a new scene has begun.
I was a stranger passing time, but now
that I am looking, I see

faces I recall, traces
of the Aultmans and the Lotts,
of the rowdy class I taught
the year before I left. After all
the years of self-exile,
the roots that never took
elsewhere, when I am motherless,
is this what I will need?

The air that sweats and weeps,
soothes the edges
from our faces. The clouds
approaching. The walls around me.

Calling

In the dream I asked for,
priests lined up like a receiving line
in front of my parents' house. I begged,
"What does this have to do
with me?" The sky
gave the word: *Contemplate*.
I looked up to receive it.

Then I left that house,
my father in his favorite flannel shirt
waving good-bye from the carport,
my mother inside rocking a grandchild
to avoid speaking that word.
I put the Appalachian Trail between us.
Set down first them, then one old friend
and another, laying blocks to build
the walls of my enclosure and obey
the call to silence, closing
my eyes on the world.

Back on the steps
of my parents' house again
as my mother lies dying, I remember
the dream. The yard holds no more
priests, no divine messages,
only the faintest echo
of my father's whistle
heard there even the summer he died.
The creak of his swing now moved
to my brother's yard. From
the house, a hint of baking
my mother's last Italian Cream cake.

I missed all that, and more.
My nephew's wedding. The planting
of blueberry bushes. The cutting down
of the hateful chestnut tree. It has all gone
on without me. The dream,

the word—What if
I got it all wrong?
What if it meant *Look around?*

I Take It Back
> *for my brother John, 1949–91*

The last thing I said to you, the one other
time we faced each other alone.

I the only visitor, privileged past
the ward's swinging doors closed
to us on Sunday afternoon visits
fenced into the neutral ground
where we circled you, held
your attention with the only things that could
make you laugh. "I scream. You scream.
We all scream for ice cream!" I still feel
the half pint riding on my lap.
And Barq's Rootbeer
poured over it. "Burp the baby!"

My brother, lost to us from the first
too-late breath, delivered to live
all your borrowed decades within such walls as these,
where your familiar nurse now brings you to me,
legs folded under you in the wide, blue seat
of the wheelchair, your bony knees touching mine
when I pull you close. Her square hand holds on
a reassuring moment, strokes your buzzed head
as she leaves us in this room big
and empty as a midweek church.

You fidget and frown
at this interruption of what you know
of happiness. I am comforted to see
you'd rather be where you are. I tell you
that, along with other things—the sunlight
putting down stakes among the pines
peering in the wide windows, like a mural
of tired soldiers, the fight over, the hero gone
quiet now the way you settle
into the hum of my voice, the holding
of your hand, like a grounding wire.

I tell you why I've come. How
they said you've outlived yourself
now, systems weakened, time
running out, our mother said. Here
I am. My words to you just a hiss
of water over rocks spilling
secrets I didn't even know
until I heard them speak. Suddenly

it all comes out. I tell you
Mother loved you best after all.
It wasn't your fault she sent you away.
I was born. I am sorry. Only
you might have held the rip in her heart
tight enough to shut out the cold.
All my life I, too, have missed you
as if we were twins, one of us stillborn.

That much was true. These things I thought
you'd want to hear. You seemed to
listen, though it might have been the way
I rubbed your arms the whole time
you sat still for, my whispers
like flies buzzing, small price to pay.

I said one thing more as
if it too might comfort: *You
haven't missed much*. Grief
an empty hammock
you and I held up our ends of.
Its weight suddenly doubled.

Or I said it like confession
on a deathbed, albeit yours. Ours now,
no secret safer than told
to a priest with twice-sealed lips.

Or I thought I could hand it off.
You could take it away. A hostage
cry for help stowed in your passage. Or a voice
that might stop echoing in your grave.

That last thing I said, I didn't mean
to hurt you. That, lying
next to you forever. I thought
it couldn't matter. You were safe
from me. Then I remembered

the only thing you ever spoke, the words
you heard over and over before
you went away, called to me
night after night in my crib
as even then I resisted sleep so often
you learned to mimic the family
chorus. "Shush, girl!"
No surprise, then, this familiar cry
this secret whispered now. You've always known.

Know this. I wasn't lying.
But I was wrong. I take it back, that moan
void as the blind crawl of crawfish
tracing the cracked map of a dry pond bed.

You and I. We missed it. Everything
so far. I have learned this just lately, seeing
the sun watch over my village and its ocean
as it was doing all along, without me. You
must also know it now, if truth-telling figures in
at all. Knowing, you will understand
as I lay down my end of that hammock and go
shopping for raspberries and almonds,
avocados, lamb, and wine. A friend
is coming for dinner at sunset,
and I don't want to miss it.

For Once

It was just
the two of us in the house, quiet
and still open to light. You
at the sewing machine
like a bird mending her nest,
and I, at your feet
on cool, hard tile among remnants,
the spring catalog open
to the mother-daughter dresses
you were making us.

You have forgotten it,
and I had forgotten why I remembered
until I went looking for something,
anything, I could thank you for
before you die.

I found this at least
once, I had you to myself,
could see that you were trying
to make something whole
of all the pieces.

Leavings
> *for my mother*

When the phone rings, this time
I know it is not the wind chimes
waking me. I leave the lights off,
making the news wait

until morning. I see you still alive,
many years ago, in the pink light
of your bedroom window, listening to me
carry on about a Wallace Stevens poem.

You folded your hands as if
to hold what might have been
a child and whispered,
this time without sarcasm,

what I wish I could say
to you now: There is so much
I would never have known
if not for you.

VI

Manmade
> *for my grandmother Pearl*

I can almost see the cardboard suitcase
you sat on in the middle of the narrow road
like a scar between fallow fields.

You wear an old black coat tight for your tall frame.
In the picture I imagine
you are on your way

to meet your beau—
you never told me his name—
coming home for you.

But then I see your face
is spare and stripped like the trees
and understand this

is the trip home,
the train arriving empty
and no other due.

A farmer's wagon took you
this far back. Yes, you whispered,
your journey had been hard as unplowed ground.

Your pa found you here, like he knew
to look. Back home
he nodded once

setting down your suitcase.
You went back
to cooking and cleaning,

splashing your morning face
with cold water like your mama
told you to before she died

to keep roses on your cheeks.
Though so did the woodstove's heat,
water boiling for laundry,

bean picking, pie making
in the middle of the day.
Never asking why

the train was empty, no one
told you but pity
in the eyes

on Sunday at church—
poor thing's one chance lost
to the Great War.

~

Later, like your daddy, Widower George
admired those roses on your face and wanted you
to run his big place a few miles over.

He knocked on the kitchen door.
"Miss? Your daddy said I could
have you." I imagine you

stiffened a little if not a lot, maybe grunted
in that way you have to stop
things at your throat.

He didn't expect an answer
to what no one had asked. You
packed your favorite apron

collaged with berry stains.
Your favorite cooking spoon,
the best knife. Your dowry.

Your other dress.
Your gardening shoes.
You tucked the piece of lace

you'd carried in your suitcase
deep inside your mama's bible
to remind you of your place.

~

I'm imagining all this too.
The old man—I'll say it:
Grandpa—taking you to his bed nights

while his daughter slipped
out her bedroom window
to meet the town boy at the river.

Never mind
the sons who came and went
bold and noisy through the front door

no questions asked. Come late spring,
after the garden was in the ground,
your own first boy came. The second,

the next year on a July day
after you'd picked tomatoes
and heard the last jar seal.

Like my father, he seemed to know
work came first. The next year,
another, and the next.

I know what I know
from the fragments you showed me
like soap opera trailers through the years.

The rest stitched together like the scraps
from home-sewn pants you wore
for twenty years after Grandpa died, bold

black and white swirls,
navy stripes quilted
to that sale-table-green backside.

~

"Don't want no man,"
you told the widowers who called.
You tore down the drafty farmhouse

in exchange for the cheap cinderblock
with sweaty walls my uncle built for you
in exchange for everything you owned.

Daddy stopped by every day to see you
sitting on the carport swing.
He told me, you know,

that you never once hugged him
but he always knew you loved him.
Now that I think about it,

I never heard you say the word myself,
though I know how it smelled. Crisp
bacon on a Saturday morning. Fresh pressed sheets.

An Easter perm at Rita Sue's. Nadinola face cream.
In summer, blanched beans cooling,
hot fat on collard greens.

~

We never talked about this either.
The summer I took up with the local rebel.
I asked, but no one said no,

so I made a show of riding around
days on his motorcycle, evenings
in a red Firebird

that always seemed to stall
down some dark side road.
Still no one pulled me back

from that dark crack in the earth.
They left me to it.
Even you,

when you finally spoke
your disapproval, this is what you said:
"Think about your daddy."

~

I do. Every day. Sooner or later
I think of you on your narrow bed,
one bloody hand always reaching

for Psalm 63:
I meditate on thee in the night.
Because thou hast been my help.

Your front door ajar.
Daddy and Uncle Ed going in armed
with a pistol and a hammer

finding you in bed
your other hand against the wall
scrawled with exclamation marks of terror.

The man asleep there in your blood,
jerked up to Daddy's pistol in his face.
I imagine stopping on this frame.

Daddy in the balance
interrupted
by something like a voice:

Vengeance is mine, saith the Lord.
Daddy listening hard
to hear it again

as truck drivers carried the story
up and down the state
of the coward who didn't shoot

the man who killed his mama.
Listening for it
in the nightmares, in the waking

to live it all again. Eventually
in the dark tunnels of chemo,
in the relentless taunting

that razed his body
into a necessary silence
you would have understood.

Yes, I think of Daddy,
of you, this conversation
I would never want to have.

Of the resolve in your eyes
as you sat on that suitcase seeing
your future shape-shifting in the wagon's dust.

Joycelyn Trigg, a native of Mississippi, spent most of her career in Atlanta and Athens, Georgia. Now she lives in Mendocino, California.

In Hattiesburg, Mississippi, she was managing editor of the *Southern Quarterly: A Journal of the Arts in the South,* published by the University of Southern Mississippi. At the Federal Reserve Bank of Atlanta she was economics research editor and publications director for more than a decade. She finished her career at the University of Georgia as an editor and publications director; her last position there was Communications Director for Public Service and Outreach.

The same year she retired, she accomplished an MFA degree from the Rainier Writing Workshop at Pacific Lutheran University in Tacoma, Washington. She also has a Master's degree in English from the University of Southern Mississippi.

Living in Mendocino was a long-held dream. Finding a way to live there, she learned that a dream deferred is not necessarily a dream denied. In Mendocino she has taught at the coast campus of College of the Redwoods and worked as a freelance editor. But she has mostly focused on writing, and poetry is her first love. She enjoys living in the creative atmosphere of Mendocino and participates in the vibrant local writing community.

But Mississippi and the Deep South run deep, and her history there often prompts her writing, as it does in *Vital Records,* a collection of poems that mostly grew out of her life there, lived and imagined.

www.ingramcontent.com/pod-product-compliance
Lightning Source LLC
Chambersburg PA
CBHW030055170426
43197CB00010B/1538